All Scripture references taken from the KJV of the Holy Bible, unless otherwise indicated.

Give Us This Day
by Dr. Marlene Miles
Freshwater Press 2024
freshwaterpress9@gmail.com

ISBN: 978-1-965772-28-7

Paperback Version

Table of Contents

Give Us This Day

The Lord's Prayer with Prophetic Exhortation

Freshwater Press, USA

Introduction

Recently, there was a trend in *prayer-dom* to pray the Lord's Prayer for an hour, straight. I did that and it was a very spiritual experience. I recorded it for myself but ended up uploading it to Warfare Prayer Channel on You tube to share with others. It has been a blessing to many and as well to me over and over. I play and pray with it or play it from time to time in the mornings when I wake up, or sometimes to feel better if I need Godly support. Sometimes I play it or any of the prayers on that channel to set the atmosphere in my house or workplace, whether I am home or not.

The Lord's Prayer

Our Father which art in
heaven, Hallowed be thy
name.
Thy kingdom come,
Thy will be done in earth,
as it is in heaven.
Give us this day our daily
bread.
And forgive us our debts,
as we forgive our debtors.
And lead us not into
temptation, but deliver us
from evil:
For thine is the kingdom,
and the power, and the
glory, forever.
AMEN.

Section I

Prophetic Exhortation

Give Us Bread

Lord, give us bread. Lord, give us a king. And God gives us the desires of our heart. Lord, whatever we ask, by faith we know it shall be given.

Lord, give us light that we do not grope about in the noonday.

Lord, give us help from trouble, for vain is the help from man. Lord, give us help from struggle, for vain is the help of man.

Lord, give us a king.

For unto us a child is born. Unto us, a son is given,

and the government shall be upon his shoulder, and his name shall be called Wonderful, Counselor, the mighty God, the Everlasting Father, the Prince of Peace, King of Kings, Lord of Lords.

Give us of Your oil, Lord, for our lamps have gone out.

He shall bring forth Thy righteousness as the light, and Thy judgment as the noon day. I shall not be afraid of the arrow that flies by day, nor for the wasteful destruction of the noonday.

Thank You, Lord.

Peace, He said. Jesus said, "I leave you peace. Peace, I leave with you. My peace I give unto you, not as the world giveth, give I unto you. Let not your heart be troubled, neither let it be afraid."

Thank You, Father. Where you spared not Your own

Son, but You delivered Him up for all of us.

How shall He not also give us freely all good things?

Thank You, Lord.

Your Spirit

Thank You, Lord, for you have not left us comfortless, but You've given us Your Spirit, the Comforter, our Helper, our Great Intercessor. And, Lord, You give us all things that pertain to life and to godliness.

Thank You, Lord.

Lord, let us give unto You. We give unto the Lord praise and honor and glory. We give unto the Lord.

O ye mighty give unto the Lord, glory and strength. Give unto the Lord the glory due

His name. Worship the Lord in the beauty of holiness.

O sing unto the Lord a new song. Sing unto the Lord, all the earth. Sing unto the Lord, bless his name.

Show forth his salvation from day-to-day. Declare his glory among the heathen, His wonders among the people. For the Lord is great and greatly to be praised.

He is to be feared above all *gods*.

For all the gods of the nations are idols. But the Lord made the heavens.

Honor and majesty are before him. Strength and beauty are in his sanctuary

Give unto the Lord. O ye kindreds of the people, give unto

the Lord glory and strength. Give unto the Lord the glory due unto His name.

Bring an offering and come into His courts. O worship the Lord in the beauty of holiness. Fear Him all the earth.

Say among the heathen that the Lord reigneth. The world also shall be established that it shall not be moved. He shall judge the people, righteously.

Let the heavens rejoice, and let the earth be glad. Let the sea roar, and the fullness thereof.

Let the field be joyful, and all that is therein.

Then shall all the trees of the wood rejoice before the Lord.

For He cometh to judge the earth, He shall judge the world with righteousness and the people with His Truth.

He that spared not his own son, but delivered him up for us how shall he not with Him also freely give us all things?

Bread of Heaven

And then they said unto Him, Lord, evermore, give us this bread.

Bread of Heaven. This is the bread that cometh down from heaven, that a man may eat thereof and not die.

"I am the living bread which came down from heaven. If any man eats of this bread, he shall live forever, and the bread that I will give is my flesh which I give for the life of the world," says the Lord.

Bread of life. And Jesus said unto them, I am the bread of life, he that cometh to Me shall never hunger, and he that believeth on me shall never thirst. And whatsoever you shall ask in my name, that will I do, that the Father may be glorified in the Son.

If you ask anything in my name, I will do it.

And therefore I say unto you, what things so ever you desire when you pray, believe that you receive them, and you shall have them.

And Jesus said, "In that day, you shall ask me nothing, verily, verily, I say unto you, whatsoever you shall ask the Father, in my name, he will give it to you."

Son of David

Son of David, have Mercy on me, a Sinner. Son of David, have Mercy on me, a Sinner. Son of David, have Mercy on me, a Sinner.

Jesus Christ, the Son of Man, has power on Earth to forgive sins.

Our Father which art in heaven hallowed be thy name…

Section II

Prophetic Exhortation
with Scriptures

Give Us Bread w/Scriptures

Lord, give us bread.

And when money failed in the land of Egypt and in the land of Canaan, all the Egyptians came unto Joseph, and said, Give us bread for why should we die in thy presence? For the money faileth. (Genesis 47:15)

Give Us a King
w/Scriptures

Lord, give us a king.

And God gives us the desires of our heart. Lord, whatever we ask--, it shall be given.

And whatsoever ye shall ask in my name, that will I do, that the Father may be glorified in the Son. [14] If ye shall ask any thing in my name, I will do it.
John 14:13-14

Therefore, I say unto you, what things so ever ye desire when ye pray, believe that ye receive them, and ye shall have them.

And in that day ye shall ask me nothing. Verily, verily, I say unto you, Whatsoever ye shall ask the Father in my name, he will give it you." (John 16:23)

Give Us Light w/Scriptures

Lord, give us light that we do not grope about in the noonday.

And he shall bring forth thy righteousness as the light, and thy judgment as the noonday.
(Psalm 37:6)

I shall not be afraid of the arrow that flies by day, nor the wasteful destruction of the noonday.
(Psalm 91:16)

Give Us Help w/Scriptures

Lord, give us help from trouble, for vain is the help from man. Lord, give us help from struggle, for vain is the help of man.

Give us help from trouble: for vain is the help of man.
(Psalm 60:11)

Give us help from trouble: for vain is the help of man.
(Psalm 108:12)

Lord, Give Us a King
w/Scriptures

Lord, give us a king.

But the thing displeased Samuel, when they said, Give us a king to judge us, And Samuel prayed unto the Lord. (1 Samuel 8:6)

For unto us a child is born unto us, a son is given, and the government shall be upon his shoulder, and his name shall be called Wonderful, Counselor, the Mighty God, the Everlasting Father, the Prince of Peace, King of Kings, Lord of Lords. (Isaiah 9:6)

THEN GOD GAVE US JESUS – UNTO US A CHILD IS BORN, A SON IS GIVEN.

For unto us a child is born, unto us a son is given: and the government shall be upon his shoulder: and his name shall be called Wonderful, Counsellor, The mighty God, The everlasting Father, The Prince of Peace. Isaiah 9:6

KING of Kings, LORD of Lords.

Which in his times he shall shew, who is the blessed and only Potentate, the King of kings, and Lord of lords. (1 Timothy 6:15)

They will wage war against the Lamb, but the Lamb will triumph over them because he is Lord of lords and King of kings—and with him will be his called, chosen and faithful followers. (Revelations 17:14)

And he hath on his vesture and on his thigh a name written, KING OF KINGS, AND LORD OF LORDS (Revelations 19:16)

Give Us Oil w/Scriptures

Give us of Your oil, Lord, for our lamps have gone out.

And the foolish said unto the wise, give us of your oil; for our lamps are gone out. (Matthew 25:8)

He shall bring forth Thy righteousness as the light, and Thy judgment as the noon day. I shall not be afraid of the arrow that flies by day, nor for the wasteful destruction of the noonday.

Thou shalt not be afraid of the terror by night, nor of the arrow that flieth by day,

nor of the pestilence that
walketh in darkness, nor of the
destruction that layeth waste at
noonday. (Psalm 91:5-6)

Thank You, Lord.

Give Us Peace
w/Scriptures

Peace, He said. Jesus said, "I leave you peace. Peace, I leave with you, My peace I give unto you not as the world giveth, give I unto you. Let not your heart be troubled, neither let it be afraid." (John 14:27)

Thank You, Father. Where you spared not Your own Son, but You delivered Him up for all of us.

How shall He not also give us freely all good things?

Thank You, Lord.

He that spared not his own Son, but delivered him up for us,

how shall he not with him also
freely give us all things?
(Romans 8:32)

Your Spirit w/Scriptures

Thank You, Lord, for you have not left us comfortless, but You've given us Your Spirit, the Comforter, our Helper, our Great Intercessor. And, Lord, you give us all things that pertain to life and to godliness.

He has not left us comfortless, but He has given us His SPIRIT, the Comforter, our Helper, our great intercessor.

According as his divine power hath given unto us all things that pertain unto life and godliness, through the knowledge of him that hath called us to glory and virtue:
(2 Peter 1:3)

Let us give unto You.

Give unto the Lord…
praise and honor and Glory.

Give unto the LORD, O ye
mighty, give unto the LORD
glory and strength. Give unto
the LORD the glory due unto
his name; Worship the LORD in
the beauty of holiness. (Psalm
29:1-2)

Psalm 96

O sing unto the LORD a new song: sing unto the LORD, all the earth.

Sing unto the Lord, bless his name, shew forth his salvation from day to day.

Declare his glory among the heathen, his wonders among all people.

For the LORD is great, and greatly to be praised: he *is* to be feared above all gods.

For all the gods of the nations are idols: but the LORD made the heavens.

Honour and majesty are before him: strength and beauty are in his sanctuary.

Give unto the LORD, O ye kindreds of the people, give unto the LORD glory and strength.

Give unto the LORD the glory due unto his name: bring an offering, and come into his courts.

O worship the LORD in the beauty of holiness: fear before him, all the earth.

Say among the heathen that the LORD reigneth: the world also shall be established that it shall not be moved: he shall judge the people righteously.

Let the heavens rejoice and let the earth be glad, le the sea roar, and the fulness therof.

Let the field be joyful, and all that is therein; then shall all the trees of the wood rejoice.

Thank You, Lord.

He that spared not his own son, but delivered him up for us how shall he not with Him also freely give us all things?

Bread of Heaven w/ Scriptures

And then they said unto Him, Lord, evermore, give us this bread.

Bread of Heaven. This is the bread that cometh down from heaven, that a man may eat thereof and not die.

I am the living bread which came down from heaven. If any man eat of this bread, he shall live forever, and the bread that I will give is my flesh which I give for the life of the world, says the Lord.

Bread of life. And Jesus said unto them, "I am the bread of life, he that cometh to Me shall never hunger, and he that believeth on me shall never thirst. And whatsoever you shall ask in my name, that will I do, that the Father may be glorified in the Son."

If you ask the Father anything in my Name, I will do it. Therefore, I say unto you, whatsoever things ye desire when ye pray, believe that ye receive them and ye shall have them. And Jesus said in that day ye shall ask me nothing, verily, verily I say unto you, whatsoever ye ask the Father in my Name He will give it to you. (Mark 11:24)

Son of David w/Scriptures

Son of David, have Mercy on me, a Sinner. Son of David, have Mercy on me, a Sinner. Son of David, have Mercy on me, a Sinner.

And he cried, saying, Jesus, thou son of David, have mercy on me. (Luke 18:38)

Jesus Christ, the Son of Man, has power on Earth to forgive sins.

But that ye may know that the Son of man hath power upon earth to forgive sins, (he said unto the sick of the palsy,) I say unto thee, Arise, and take up thy couch, and go into thine house. (Luke 5:24)

Our Father which art in heaven hallowed be thy name...

Forgive Us Our Trespasses

Our Father which art in
heaven, Hallowed be thy name.
Thy kingdom come,
They will be done in earth, as it
is in heaven.
Give us this day our daily
bread.
And forgive us our trespasses as
we forgive those who trespass
against us.
And lead us not into temptation,
but deliver us from evil:
For thine is the kingdom, and
the power, and the glory,
forever.
AMEN.

In Earth or *On* Earth

There are versions of the Lord's Prayer, so I've added another version just before this Appendix. Also, someone once contacted me to discuss, *in Earth* versus *on Earth*. In Earth can indicate in the realm of the Earth, not inside of the Earth. God is particular about many things, but it is the Holy Spirit who helps us to pray. Find out if God is particular about this or not.

Upon research, I discovered that the King James Version reads, *on Earth* and other translations read *in Earth*.

I learned the Lord's Prayer as a child and when you pray the Lord's Prayer once or for an hour, you will, most likely, default to how you learned it, as I surely do. Ask the Lord what is the correct version for you to pray and pray that version. Amen.

Luke 11:1-4

And it came to pass, that, as he was praying in a certain place, when he ceased, one of his disciples said unto him, Lord, teach us to pray, as John also taught his disciples.

And he said unto them, When ye pray, say, Our Father which art in heaven, Hallowed be thy name. Thy kingdom come. Thy will be done, as in heaven, so in earth.

Give us day by day our daily bread.

And forgive us our sins; for we also forgive every one that is indebted to us. And lead us not

into temptation; but deliver us
from evil.

As you may be now aware, Matthew's version of the Lord's Prayer is most often used and is the full prayer not an abbreviated version as the one in the Gospel according to Luke.

Testimony

.   I prayed the Lord's Prayer 100 times (or more), for several days, and recorded it for future use, but decided to share it as a video on Warfare Prayer Channel (You Tube).

I was on day three of praying The Lord's Prayer 100+ times and then waiting on the Lord. On the third night doing so, I fell asleep, and in the dream, I was at work, preparing for the day to start, where there are numerous computer monitors. The Lord's prayer was playing on what I thought was one of them, in my voice.

When it was time for business hours to start, I thought it would be best to turn off the sound, since it was kind of loud, but it would not turn off.

The first customers who came into the business was a couple that I know and love, and I know that they are saved. They were dressed beautifully like Sunday morning for church. They were fine with the Lord's Prayer playing because we couldn't turn it off.

I asked staff members to help me turn the sound off. There were 4 different people there, but I think only one person offered any help. Still, they could not turn it off-- it kept playing; it was wonderful.

That's when I realized in the dream it is playing on EVERY monitor in the business. We still kept trying to turn it off, even unplugging one of the monitors from electricity -- it kept playing. Another monitor was ripped from the wall completely, but it kept playing.

The prayers of the saints never fail. The prayers of the saints live on. The prayers of the saints resound through the Earth, the Heavens and throughout eternity. Never stop praying.

Then a "new" (unknown) staff member came with a package (some items wrapped in pink tissue paper, as a gift) and said, It's Father's Day, is this a good gift package for Father's Day?

I said, "Yes."

The package had what I believed to be 2 Hershey Kisses in it and some other items, to include a very nice coconut coffee. Looking twice I noticed the coffee had been opened and deemed that unacceptable. But I found some nice coconut coffee in a bag that had not been opened, and swapped it out for the opened coffee bag. I then stated that we will find more new coffee to put in the gift packages.

The new girl told me she had made up other gift packages as well, since it was Father's Day.

I will keep praying the Lord's Prayer. And you should as well, your prayers will reach Heaven and they will echo and resound throughout time and space.

Praise the Lord, and
Amen.

This book represents a transcript of the spoken prayer that is on You Tube Warfare Prayer Channel https://www.youtube.com/watch?v=j2HcoJv7GXM&t=2754s That video is entitled, ***Give Us This Day.***

Dear Reader

Thank you for acquiring, reading, and sharing this book.

Our Father is gracious and faithful; He will give all things that pertain to your life and godliness. Seek Him daily.

In the Name of Jesus,

Amen.

Dr. Marlene Miles

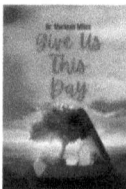

Prayer books by this author

While most books by this author have
prayer points either throughout the book
or at the end, there are some books that
are **only** prayers. You just open up the
book and pray. They are listed below:

Prayers Against Barrenness: *For
Success in Business and Life*

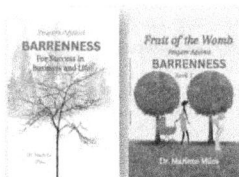

Fruit of the Womb: *Prayers Against
Barrenness*

Beauty Curses, *Warfare Prayers
Against* https://a.co/d/5Xlc20M

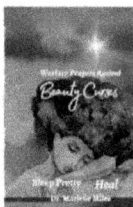

**Courts of Marriage: Prayers for
Marriage in the Courts of Heaven**
(prayerbook) https://a.co/d/cNAdgAq

Courtroom Warfare @ Midnight
(prayerbook) https://a.co/d/5fc7Qdp

Demonic Cobwebs *(prayerbook)*
https://a.co/d/fp9Oa2H

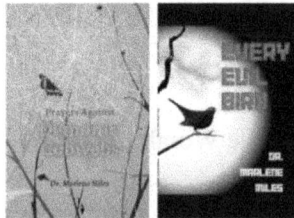

Every Evil Bird
https://a.co/d/hF1kh1O

Every Evil Arrow
https://a.co/d/afgRkiA

Gates of Thanksgiving

Give Us This Day

Spirits of Death & the Grave, Pass Over Me and My House
https://a.co/d/dS4ewyr

*Please note that my name is spelled
incorrectly on amazon, but not on the
book.*

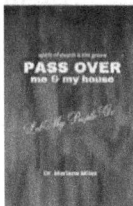

Throne of Grace: Courtroom
Prayer

https://a.co/d/fNMxcM9

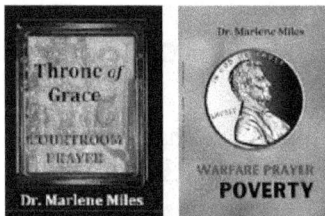

Warfare Prayer Against Poverty
https://a.co/d/bZ61lYu

Other books by this author
AK: *The Adventures of the Agape Kid*

AMONG SOME THIEVES

Ancestral Powers
https://a.co/d/9prTyFf

Anti-Marriage, *The Spirit of*

Backstabbers
https://a.co/d/gi8iBxf

Barrenness, *Prayers Against*
https://a.co/d/feUltIs

Battlefield of Marriage, *The*

Blindsided: *Has the Old Man Bewitched You?*
https://a.co/d/5O2fLLR

Break Free from Collective Captivity

Casting Down Imaginations
https://a.co/d/1UxlLqa

Evil Touch
https://a.co/d/gSGGpS1

Failed Assignment
https://a.co/d/3CXtjZY

Fantasy Spirit Spouse
https://a.co/d/hW7oYbX

FAT Demons (The): *Breaking Demonic Curses*

The Fold (5-book series)

- The Fold (Book 1)
- Name Your Seed (Book 2)
- The Poor Attitudes of Money (3)
- Do Not Orphan Your Seed (4)
- For the Sake of the Gospel (5)
- My Sowing Journal

Gang Ups: *Touch Not God's Anointed*

Give Us This Day

got HEALING? Verses for Life

got LOVE? Verses for Life

got HOPE? Verses for Life

got money?
https://a.co/d/g2av41N

How to Dental Assist

How to Dental Assist2: Be
Productive, Not Wasteful

I Take It Back

It's Coming Back: *Vengeance Is the
Lord's, So Stop Making Weapons*

Legacy

Let Me Have A Dollar's Worth
https://a.co/d/h8F8XgE

Let Them Come Up & Worship

Level the Playing Field

Living for the NOW of God

Lose My Location
https://a.co/d/crD6mV9

Man Safari, *The*

Marriage Ed. Rules of Engagement
& Marriage

Made Perfect in Love

Money Hunters: Beware of Those

Money on the Altar
https://a.co/d/4EqJ2Nr

Mulberry Tree
https://a.co/d/9nR9rRb

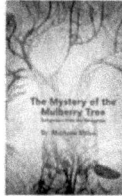

Motherboard (The) - *Soul Prosperity Series*

Name Your Seed

Occupy: *Until I Return*

Plantation Souls

Players Gonna Play

Power Money: Nine Times the Tithe

https://a.co/d/gRt41gy

The Power of Wealth *(forthcoming)*

Powers Above

Remember the Time
https://a.co/d/3PbBjkF

Repent of Visiting Evil Altars
https://a.co/d/3n3Zjwx

The Robe, *Part 1, The Lessons of Joseph*

The Robe, *The Lessons of Joseph* Part II,

Seasons of Grief

Seasons of Waiting

Seasons of War

Second Marriage, Third--, *Any Marriage*

https://a.co/d/6m6GN4N

Seducing Spirits: *Idolatry & Whoredoms*

Sift You Like Wheat

Six Men Short: What Has Happened to all the Men?

Soul Prosperity, Soul Prosperity Series Book 3 https://a.co/d/5p8YvCN

Soulish & Diabolical Prayer Treatment

Souls In Captivity, Soul Prosperity Series Book 2

The Spirit of Anti-Marriage

The Spirit of Poverty

StarStruck

SUNBLOCK

The Swallowers: *Thieves of Darkness*, Book 3

Take It Back

This Is NOT That: How to Keep Demons from Coming at You

Time Is of the Essence

Too Many Wives: *Why You Have Lady Problems*

Tormenting Spirits
https://a.co/d/dAogEJf

Toxic Souls

Triangular Power *(series)*

- Powers Above
- SUNBLOCK
- Do Not Swear by the Moon
- STARSTRUCK

Uncontested Doom

Unguarded Hours, *The*

Unseen Life, *The*
https://a.co/d/0drZ5Ll

Unstable As Water: *Thou Shalt Not Excel*

Upgrade: How to Get Out of Survival Mode

- Toxic Souls (Book 2 of series)
- Legacy (Book 3 of series)

The Wasters: *Thieves of Darkness,* Bk 2 https://a.co/d/bUvI9Jo

What Have You to Declare? What Do You Have With You from Where You've Been?

When I Was A Child, *I Prayed As a Child*

When the Devourer is Rebuked

https://a.co/d/1HVv8oq

The Wilderness Romance *(series)*
This series is about conducting a Godly relationship and marriage with someone who is a Wilderness person. It is about how to recognize it and navigate through it. These books are about how not to get caught up in such.

- *The Social Wilderness*
- *The Sexual Wilderness*

- *The Spiritual Wilderness*

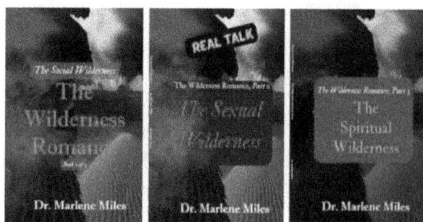

Other Series

The Fold (a series on Godly finances)
https://a.co/d/4hz3unj

Soul Prosperity Series
https://a.co/d/bz2M42q

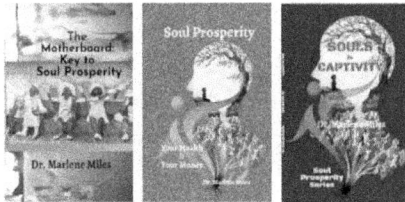

Spirit Spouse books

https://a.co/d/9VehDSo

https://a.co/d/97sKOwm

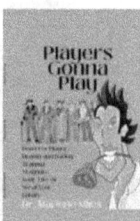

Thieves of Darkness series

Triangular Powers
https://a.co/d/aUCjAWC

Upgrade (series) *How to Get Out of Survival Mode* https://a.co/d/aTERhXO

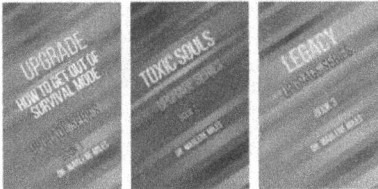

www.ingramcontent.com/pod-product-compliance
Lightning Source LLC
Chambersburg PA
CBHW060040040426
42331CB00032B/1944